T0210276

SCHIRMER'S LIBRARY
OF MUSICAL CLASSICS

Vol. 309

CORNELIUS GURLITT

Op. 101

Albumleaves
for the Young

Twenty Little Pieces
For the Piano

ISBN 978-0-7935-5225-2

G. SCHIRMER, Inc.

DISTRIBUTED BY

HAL•LEONARD®
CORPORATION

7777 W. BLUEMOUND RD. P.O. BOX 13819 MILWAUKEE, WI 53213

Printed in the U.S.A. by G. Schirmer, Inc.

CONTENTS.

March.

Marsch.

C. Gurlitt. Op. 101.

Vivace ma non troppo.

Morning Prayer.
Morgengebet.

The Sunshiny Morning.

Heiterer Morgen.

Northern Strains.

Nordische Klänge.

By the Spring.

An der Quelle.

Moderato, quasi Allegretto.

Slumber Song.
Schlummerlied.

Lament.

Klage.

C. GURLITT. Op. 101.

The Fair.

Kirmess.

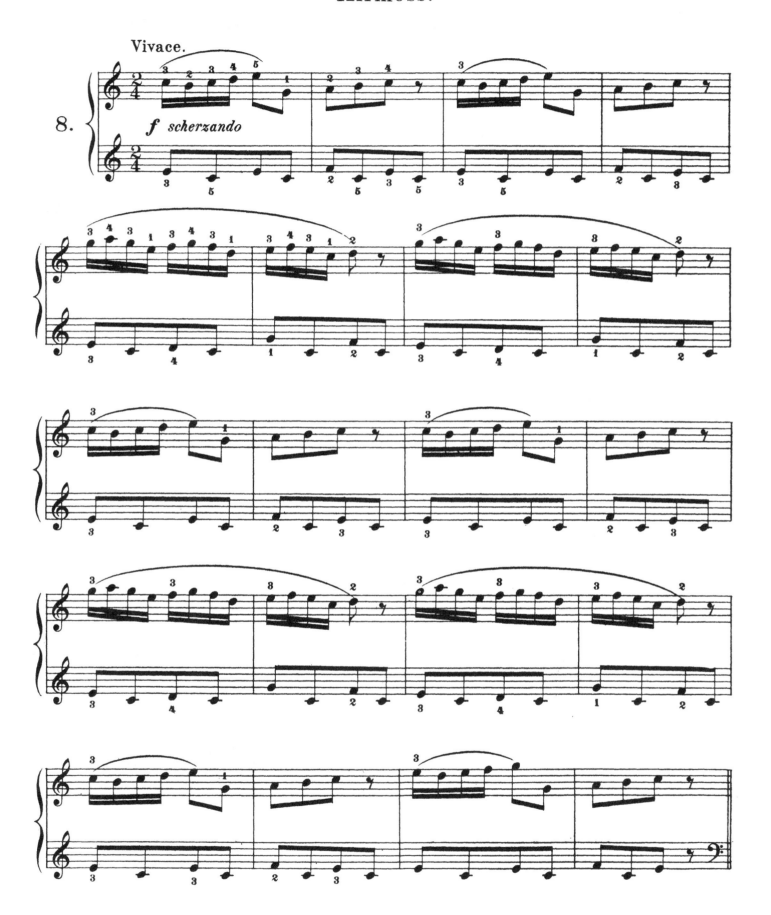

Turkish March.
Türkischer Marsch.

Song without Words.

Lied ohne Worte.

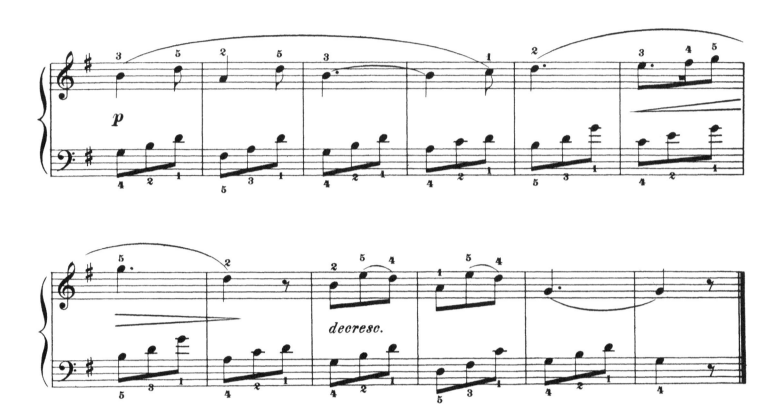

Waltz.
Walzer.

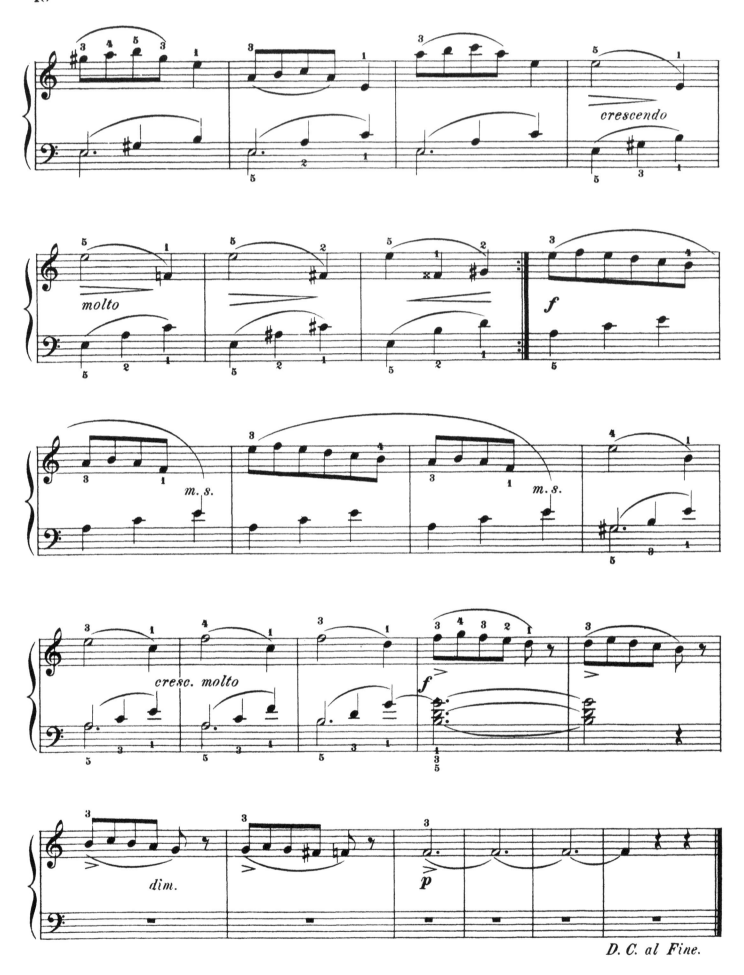

D. C. al Fine.

The little Wanderer.

Der kleine Wandersmann.

Grandfather's Birthday.

Grossvaters Geburtstag.

Valse Noble.

LOSS.
Verlust.

Scherzo.

Free Fancies.

Schwärmerei.

Sunday.
Sonntag.

Choral. { Praise the Lord, the Almighty King of Glory.
Lobe den Herren, den mächtigen König der Ehren.

Hunting Song.
Jagdstück.

Salto Mortale.

20.